BEHIND THE SCENES BIOGRAPHIES

WHAT YOU NEVER KNEW ABOUT

>>>—————————————————<<<

SIMONE BILES

by Helen Cox Cannons

CAPSTONE PRESS

a capstone imprint

Published by Spark, an imprint of Capstone
1710 Roe Crest Drive, North Mankato, Minnesota 56003
capstonepub.com

Library of Congress Cataloging-in-Publication Data
Names: Cox Cannons, Helen- author.
Title: Simone Biles : gymnastics legend / by Helen Cox Cannons.
Description: North Mankato, Minnesota : Capstone Press, A Capstone Imprint, [2023] | Series: Behind the Scenes Bios | Includes bibliographical references and index. | Audience: Ages 8-11 | Audience: Grades 4-6 | Summary: "Simone Biles has inspired the world with her incredible gymnastics achievements, including her many Olympic medals. But what is her life like outside of the gym? High-interest details and bold photos of her exciting life will enthrall reluctant and struggling readers, while carefully leveled text will leave them feeling confident."— Provided by publisher.
Identifiers: LCCN 2020037776 (print) | LCCN 2020037777 (ebook) | ISBN 9781666356809 (hardcover) | ISBN 9781669040170 (paperback) | ISBN 9781666356816 (pdf) | ISBN 9781666356830 (kindle edition)
Subjects: LCSH: Biles, Simone, 1997—-Juvenile literature. | Gymnasts—United States—Biography—Juvenile literature. | Women gymnasts—United States—Biography—Juvenile literature.
Classification: LCC GV460.2.B55 B65 2021 (print) | LCC GV460.2.B55 (ebook) | DDC 796.44092 [B]—dc23
LC record available at https://lccn.loc.gov/2020037776
LC ebook record available at https://lccn.loc.gov/2020037777

Editorial Credits
Editor: Mandy Robbins; Designer: Heidi Thompson; Media Researcher: Jo Miller; Production Specialist: Tori Abraham

Image Credits
Alamy: ITAR-TASS News Agency, 19, UPI, 21; Associated Press: David J. Phillip, 8; Getty Images: BEN STANSALL, 15, Carmen Mandato, 29, David Livingston, 23, Emma McIntyre, 14, GREG BAKER, 10, Kyodo News, 25, picture alliance, 5, Robert Gauthier, 17; Newscom: Tom Weller/dpa/picture-alliance, Cover; Shutterstock: A.RICARDO, 27, Boris Ryaposov, 13 (back), DFree, 7, Featureflash Photo Agency, 28, Leonard Zhukovsky, 18, LittleMiss, 22, Roschetzky Photography, 12, SEE D JAN, 13 (front), stoklaima, 16, Tartila, 7 (scale design element), grey_and, 8-9, Tinseltown, 7 (inset)

◇ ◇ ◇ ◇ ◇ ◇ ◇ ◇ ◇ ◇ ◇ ◇ ◇ ◇ ◇ ◇ ◇ ◇ ◇

TABLE OF CONTENTS

Words in **bold** are in the glossary.

◇ ◇ ◇ ◇ ◇ ◇ ◇ ◇ ◇ ◇ ◇ ◇ ◇ ◇ ◇ ◇ ◇ ◇ ◇ ◇

HOW WELL DO YOU KNOW THE
G.O.A.T.?

Simone Biles is the Greatest Of All Time! She has 32 World Championship medals. Nineteen are gold. She also has seven Olympic medals. Four of them are gold.

Greatest

Of

All

Time

What else is there to know about Simone? Let's find out!

Are you Simone's biggest fan?

Can you name her:

1. Favorite color?

2. Celebrity crush?

3. Height?

4. Nickname?

5. What makes her laugh the most?

1. Purple **2.** Zac Efron **3.** 4 feet 8 inches

4. $imoney **5.** People tripping!

7

SIMONE'S
FAVES

Simone's favorite food might be the same as yours. It's pepperoni pizza. She loves Imo's Pizza in St. Louis, Missouri. After the Olympics in 2021, Imo's sent pizza to Simone at her home in Texas.

Simone loves shopping too. Where is her favorite place to shop? Trick question! She shops online.

"I online shop a lot. It's a bad habit. A lot. If I get bored, I'm online shopping."
—Simone Biles (*Fashionista*, March 29, 2019)

SIMONE
BY THE NUMBERS

1997

6.9

Simone was born on March 14, 1997. She started gymnastics when she was 6 years old. At age 16, she won her first World Championship.

Simone has big numbers on social media. She has 1.7 million followers on Twitter. She has at least 6.9 million Instagram followers!

HOME AND
FAMILY

Houston, Texas

Celebs often have multimillion-dollar homes. Not Simone! Her house in Houston cost $750,000. It has four bedrooms, a large **patio**, and a pool.

When Simone was 6, her grandparents, Nellie and Ronald Biles, **adopted** her. She calls them Mom and Dad.

Adria and Nellie Biles

Simone's younger sister, Adria, is her biggest cheerleader. Adria was also a gymnast. They even look alike!

FACT

Adria is several inches taller than Simone. But fans often go up to Adria thinking she is Simone!

Who completes Simone's family? Her French bulldogs, Lilo and Rambo. They have their own Instagram account. It has over 86,000 followers.

FACT

There is an app called Simoji. It has Simone as cartoon gymnast figures. Her favorite emoji is the winking smiley face with its tongue sticking out.

A fan holding cutouts of Simone's dogs

FACT

Simone's house even has a dog-wash station.

NEW **MOVES**

Simone is a natural gymnast. As a young child, she did backflips off of mailboxes.

As a pro, she has invented four new moves. She invented two moves on the floor and one on both the vault and beam. They are all named "The Biles."

STYLE
QUEEN

Simone adds flare to her **leotards**. When she was practicing for the 2020 Olympics, her leo was black and gold. It had "USA" spelled out in **crystals**. Simone added a **rhinestone** goat to it. Guess why?

Simone doesn't just wear leotards. She has real fashion game. She stunned at the **Met Gala** in 2021. Six men helped her carry her dress.

2021 Met Gala

In 2017, Simone wore heels. She was on the TV show *Dancing with the Stars*. She was nervous about dancing in heels. Of course, she rocked it. She and her partner took fourth place.

FACT

Simone got a perfect score for her jive and rumba dances on the show.

SIMONE'S CHALLENGES

Simone has ADHD. This disorder affects the brain. It makes it hard to sit still and pay attention. Simone has proven that you can have ADHD and still be a pro.

"Having ADHD and taking medicine for it is nothing to be ashamed of."
—Simone Biles (Twitter, September 13, 2016)

In 2021, Simone suffered from the "**twisties**." It happened during the vault final at the 2020 Tokyo Olympics. She felt lost in the air while flipping and twisting. Simone pulled out of the individual all-round final.

As usual, Simone stayed positive. She showed people that good mental health is important.

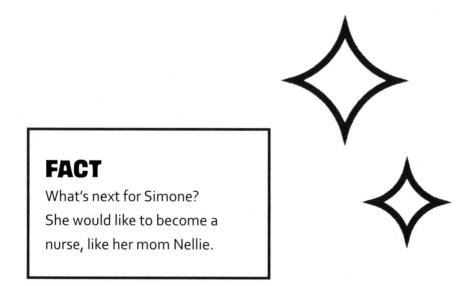

FACT

What's next for Simone? She would like to become a nurse, like her mom Nellie.

"My mental and physical health is above all medals I could ever win."

—Simon Biles (Twitter, August 19, 2021)

BESTIES!

Aly Raisman

Jordan Chiles

No matter what Simone is going through, her besties have her back! Who are two of her closest pals? Gymnasts Aly Raisman and Jordan Chiles. They've wrapped each other's ankles. They've posted selfies together too. These ladies are tight.

Glossary

adopt (uh-DOPT)—to make a child a legal part of a family

crystal (KRISS-tahl)—very high-quality glass

leotard (LEE-uh-tard)—a snug, one-piece garment worn by gymnasts

Met Gala (MET GAL-uh)—an annual fundraising event for the Metropolitan Museum of Art's Costume Institute in New York City

patio (PAT-ee-oh)—a paved area outside a house used for dining or relaxing

rhinestone (RINE-stone)—a plastic jewel used in crafts and jewelry making

twisties (TWISS-teez)—in gymnastics, a feeling of being lost in the air while performing a move; it can be very dangerous for a gymnast

Read More

Berglund, Bruce. *Olympic GOATs: The Greatest Athletes of All Time.* North Mankato, MN: Capstone Press, 2022.

Schwartz, Heather E. *Simone Biles: Greatest of All Time.* Minneapolis: Lerner Publications, 2023.

Simons, Lisa M. Bolt. *Simone Biles: Gymnastics Legend.* North Mankato, MN: Capstone Press, 2021.

Internet Sites

Simone Biles
simonebiles.com

Team USA: Simone Biles
teamusa.org/usa-gymnastics/athletes/simone-biles

Time 2021 Athlete of the Year
time.com/athlete-of-the-year-2021-simone-biles/

Index

About the Author

Helen Cox Cannons was born in Dumfriesshire, Scotland. She has a Master's Degree in English Literature from the University of Edinburgh. She has worked as an editor and author for over 25 years. In her spare time, Helen likes to crochet, sing, go for country walks, and fuss over her two cats, Nero and Diego. She lives in Witney, Oxfordshire, with her two daughters, Abby and Serena.